EXTREME NATURE

FEARSOME FORCES OF NATURE

Anita Ganeri

Raintree

Schools Library and Information Services

www.raintreepublishers.co.uk
Visit our website to find out more information about Raintree books.

To order:
☏ Phone 0845 6044371
🖹 Fax +44 (0) 1865 312263
🖥 Email myorders@raintreepublishers.co.uk

Customers from outside the UK please telephone +44 1865 312262

Raintree is an imprint of Capstone Global Library Limited, a company incorporated in England and Wales having its registered office at 7 Pilgrim Street, London, EC4V 6LB – Registered company number: 6695582

Text © Capstone Global Library Limited 2013
First published in hardback in 2013
Paperback edition first published in 2014
The moral rights of the proprietor have been asserted.

Edited by Dan Nunn, Rebecca Rissman, and Catherine Veitch
Designed by Cynthia Della-Rovere
Picture research by Tracy Cummins
Production by Alison Parsons
Originated by Capstone Global Library
Printed and bound in China by CTPS

ISBN 978 1 406 23788 7 (hardback)
16 15 14 13 12
10 9 8 7 6 5 4 3 2 1

ISBN 978 1 406 23793 1 (paperback)
17 16 15 14 13
10 9 8 7 6 5 4 3 2 1

British Library Cataloguing in Publication Data
Ganeri, Anita
Fearsome forces of nature. -- (Extreme nature)
551.2-dc22
A full catalogue record for this book is available from the British Library.

Acknowledgements
We would like to thank the following for permission to reproduce photographs: AP Photo p. 9 (Pat Roque); Corbis pp. 5 (© KYODO/REUTERS), 12 (© Jim Wark/ Visuals Unlimited), 14 (© ROB GRIFFIT/epa), 16 (© Xinhua/Xinhua Press), 17 (© Kyodo/XinHua/Xinhua Press), 19 (© STR/epa), 23 (© Chris Hellier), 26 (© JEAN-CHRISTOPHE BOTT/epa); Getty Images pp. 4 (Art Wolfe), 6 (Peter Carsten), 8 (James P. Blair), 13 (The Asahi Shimbun), 15 (YOSHIKAZU TSUNO/AFP), 18 (HIROSHI KAWAHARA/AFP), 25 (JOSE NAVARRO/ AFP); Shutterstock pp. 22 (© Yory Frenklakh), 7 (© beboy),10 (© PavelSvoboda), 11 (© Lee Prince), 20 (© akva), 21 (© rm), 24 (© Kapu), 27 (© deepspacedave).

Cover photograph of a volcanic eruption reproduced with permission of Shutterstock (© beboy).
Background photograph of fire reproduced with permission of Shutterstock (© Mettus).

Every effort has been made to contact copyright holders of material reproduced in this book. Any omissions will be rectified in subsequent printings if notice is given to the publisher.

Disclaimer
All the Internet addresses (URLs) given in this book were valid at the time of going to press. However, due to the dynamic nature of the Internet, some addresses may have changed, or sites may have changed or ceased to exist since publication. While the author and publisher regret any inconvenience this may cause readers, no responsibility for any such changes can be accepted by either the author or the publisher.

Some words are shown in bold, **like this**. You can find out what they mean by looking in the glossary.

Contents

What are forces of nature?

Did you know that Earth has about 1,500 **active volcanoes**? Fearsome forces of nature happen all over the world. You can read more about them in this book. You can also find out what people do when nature turns nasty.

DID YOU KNOW?
Earthquakes can tear roads apart and bring down bridges.

Violent volcanoes

A **volcano** is a place where red-hot, liquid rock bursts through the surface of Earth. Below ground, the rock is called **magma**. When it reaches the surface, it is called **lava**. When a volcano **erupts**, hot gas, ash, and dust are blasted into the air.

lava

DID YOU KNOW?
Lava can reach a temperature of a scorching 1,200°C! That's 12 times hotter than boiling water!

Mount Saint Helens

Some **volcanoes erupt** quite gently. Others explode with a bang. In 1980, Mount Saint Helens in Washington state, USA, erupted. The blast was so powerful that it blew half of the mountain away.

People living near volcanoes sometimes have to be **evacuated** from their homes.

Gushing geysers

A **geyser** is a hole in the ground that spurts out steam and hot water. Red-hot rocks underground heat up the water. Then the geyser blows.

The water and steam can shoot more than 50 metres into the air. That is five times as high as a house!

11

Shaking Earth

The surface of Earth is called its **crust**. Earth's hard crust is cracked into pieces. Sometimes the pieces push and slide past each other. If this happens suddenly, an earthquake can shake the ground.

The San Andreas Fault in California, United States, lies along a crack in Earth's crust.

Earthquakes can make buildings fall down and break up roads.

DID YOU KNOW?
Most earthquakes last for less than one minute.

In February 2011, a huge earthquake struck Christchurch, in New Zealand. The city was badly damaged and 181 people were killed.

DID YOU KNOW?
Japanese children practise earthquake **drills** at school.

Terrifying tsunamis

Earthquakes under the sea cause **tsunamis**. The sudden shock moves a huge amount of water, which races across the sea in waves.

DID YOU KNOW?
A tsunami travels as fast as a jet plane at sea.

The tsunami waves get higher as they reach land.

When a **tsunami** reaches land, the waves crash onto the shore. They can flood towns, rip up trees, and sweep buildings, cars, and people away.

During the 2011 tsunami in Japan, the ground shook for around 3 to 5 minutes. Thousands of people died and millions lost their homes.

Raging rivers

Flowing water is hugely powerful. It can slowly carve through solid rock to make **canyons** and caves. It can also crash over the side of a mountain, plunging down as a waterfall.

Grand Canyon, United States

DID YOU KNOW?
Angel Falls in Venezuela is the highest waterfall in the world. It is the height of three Eiffel Towers!

Cracking coasts

Along the **coast**, waves smash hard into cliffs. The waves carry rocks and stones that wear cliffs away and carve out holes and other features.

These houses are in danger of falling into the sea.

23

Awful avalanches

An **avalanche** is a massive pile of snow that suddenly breaks loose and crashes down a mountain. An avalanche can speed downhill as fast as a racing car.

An avalanche can bury walkers, skiers, and even whole villages. Some mountain villages have special steel fences around them, to slow down any falling snow.

Avalanches can strike without any warning. People can be buried in the snow. Helicopters search for survivors from the air. On the ground, rescuers use long sticks, called snow probes, to feel for people in the snow.

DID YOU KNOW?
Many things can set off an avalanche, such as a car door being slammed.

rescue dogs also help to look for survivors.

Quiz: What am I?

Read the clues, then try to work out "What am I?". Find the answers at the bottom of page 29. But guess first!

1) I come out of a **volcano**.
I can be as hot as 1,200°C.
I start off as **magma**.
What am I?

2) I'm made of steam and hot water.
I spurt out of the ground.
I can be more than 50 metres high.
What am I?

3) I usually last for less than one minute.
I make the ground shake.
I can shake buildings down.
What am I?

4) I start off at sea.
I get higher as I reach land.
I can travel as fast as a jet plane.
What am I?

5) I can bury a whole village.
I can move as fast as a racing car.
I happen in the mountains.
What am I?

Answers:
1) lava 2) geyser 3) earthquake 4) tsunami 5) avalanche.

29

Glossary

active able to erupt at any time

avalanche massive pile of snow that crashes down a mountain

canyon deep gash in the ground, carved out by water

coast edge of the land that borders the sea

crust hard, rocky outside of Earth

drill practice for what to do in an event such as a fire or an earthquake

erupt burst or explode with lava

evacuate move out of the way of danger

geyser jet of hot water and steam that shoots out of the ground

lava magma that has come to Earth's surface

magma runny, red-hot rock underground

tsunami series of waves set off by an undersea earthquake or volcano

volcano hole in the ground where red-hot rock comes out

Books

Awesome Forces of Nature series, Louise & Richard Spilsbury (Raintree, 2010)

Graphic Natural Disasters series, Rob Shone & Gary Jeffrey (Franklin Watts, 2010)

Violent Volcanoes (Horrible Geography), Anita Ganeri (Scholastic, 2008)

Websites

environment.nationalgeographic.com/ environment/natural-disasters/forces-of-nature

A National Geographic website packed with fascinating facts and pictures about forces of nature, including an activity to make your own tornado.

kids.nationalgeographic.com/kids/stories/ spacescience/freaky-forces-of-nature

Another National Geographic website, this one focuses on 10 freaky forces of nature.

Index